The FAIRIES' ALPHABET BOOK

by
Beverlie
Manson

Doubleday & Company, Inc. Garden City, New York

To Marion...
who has never lost her Fairyland.

Library of Congress Catalog Card Number 81-43401
ISBN: 0-385-17544-2
Copyright © 1982 by Beverlie Manson
All Rights Reserved
Printed in the United States of America
First Edition

A is for Apple Fairies

The fairies are happy
that the apples are ripe
and ready to be picked,
for they have spent
many long summer days
looking after them.

B is for Butterfly Fairies

With singing and dancing,
the Butterfly Fairies teach
a young fairy to fly.

C is for Candy Fairies

These fairies build
their houses with candy
they receive as gifts.

D is for Dawn Fairy

With a touch of her wand,
the Dawn Fairy spreads
the news that another
day is breaking.
Then little fairies
rise and wash in the dew.

E
is for East Wind Fairy

Have you ever wondered
why dandelion puffs
do not last until spring?
It is because the
East Wind Fairy brushes
them with her wings
as she flies through
the autumn skies.

F

is for Firefly Fairies

Firefly Fairies brighten
the night with their
golden light.

G is for Garden Fairy

When flowers quarrel,
as they sometimes do,
the Garden Fairy
is summoned to make
them both happy again.

H is for Harvest Moon Fairy

In the cool of an autumn evening,
when our work
is done,
little fairies
gather food for
the Harvest Fairy's
feast.

I is for Ice Fairies

On a cold starry night,
if you listen very hard,
you can hear a tinkling sound,
as the Ice Fairies decorate
the land with icicles.

J is for Joy Fairies

When there is joy in the air,
buttercups glisten and
blue bells ring, but
only the fairies
can hear them.

K is for King of the Fairies

The King of the Fairies
rides like the wind
to return to his Palace
before the moon is high
and the dancing begins.

L is for Lake Fairy

As the Lake Fairy waves
her wand across the water,
ripples are tipped
with silver.

M is for Moon Beam Fairy

Sitting in a pool
of shining light,
the Moon Beam Fairy
watches over the night.

N is for Night Fairies

They light up the darkness
with their fairy lanterns,
waiting and watching
for the sun to rise.

O is for Oak Fairies

Hidden in the roots
of the big oak tree,
the Oak Fairies
love to talk for hours
and have tea.

P is for Princess of the Fairies

The Princess of the Fairies
is loved by all, for she
glows like the sun and
sparkles like the stars.

Q is for Queen of the Fairies

When the Queen of
the Fairies appears,
there is music and
dancing and cheers.

R is for Rainbow Fairies

Over the hills and far away
is the end of the rainbow,
where these fairies play.

S is for Sugar Plum Fairy

The Sugar Plum Fairy
is full of fun.
A smile from her face
and hearts are won.

T

is for Tooth Fairies

When your tooth
falls out, the
Tooth Fairies use it
to help build
their ivory tower.
They usually work
at night.

U is for Unicorn Fairy

Unicorns are as difficult
to find as fairies, but
if you are very very lucky,
you may see both.

V is for Valentine Fairies

There is great excitement
on Valentine's Day
when the fairy postman
is kept busy delivering
all the messages of love.

W

is for Water Lily Fairy

Floating on the glassy pond,
the Water Lily Fairy
watches over the fish below.

X is for Kissing Fairies

High up in the trees,
two fairies sneak a kiss.

Y is for Yule Fairy

Just before Christmas Eve,
the Yule Fairy gathers
the prettiest branches
from the winter trees.

Z is for Zoo Fairies

These fairies have made
a make-believe zoo cage
out of flower stems.
But soon they will
let the butterflies
fly away...and
so will they!